PLANT YOUR FLAG.

Magnetize Mediocre Marketing.
Captivate the Best Clients.
Become the Hunted.

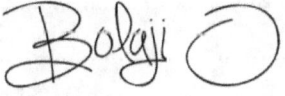

Table of Contents

Introduction 6
Chapter 1: The Chosen One. 8
    The Bachelor. 8
    LeBron James. 9
    American Idol. 11
Chapter 2: The Case Against "Me-Too" Marketing. 17
    But Who Is This For? 18
    What Keeps You Up at Night?................................... 19
    Imagine This:... 19
Chapter 3: The Signature Book. 22
    1 - One-Problem, One-Solution. 22
    2 – One Client. 25
    3 - Tightly Focused. 28
    3 - Hello, World. 30
    4 - Customer Advocate. 30
    5 - Try Before You Buy. 31
    6 - Lead Magnet. 31
    Ten Undisputable Reasons You Need a Signature Book. 32
Chapter 4: Why You Can't Wait Six More Months.......... 34
    1.   Someone needs you today: 35
    2.   You don't have to write the perfect book.......... 35

3. Imagine waiting another year, to think about that book. 36

4. Would you like a better work-life balance now, or later? 37

5. Your competition isn't waiting another twelve months. 37

Chapter 5: The F.L.A.G. Method. 39

   1. Why you Need to Plant your FLAG..................................39

   2. The Great Space Race. 39

   3. The World's Tallest Mountain..41

   4. How Does This Apply to Business? 46

   5. What is the Plant your F.L.A.G. Method? 47

Chapter 6: F: FIND the Right Book. 48

   Phase One: THE FINDING. 49

   Phase Two: THE FLESHING OUT. 68

   Phase Three: THE FINISHING. 70

Chapter 7: LAUNCH the Right Way. 73

   1. Keyword Strategy..75

   2. Category Strategy. 79

   3. Book Title, Description & Cover. 81

   4. Reviews: 84

   5. Bestseller Launch: 85

Chapter 8: ACCESS the Right Authority..88

1. 3rd-Party Credibility from Press Releases. 89

2. 3rd-Party Credibility from Interviews. 91

3. 3rd-Party Credibility from the Stage. 94

Chapter 9: GATHER the Right Clients. 97

1. Lead Magnet. 97

2. Lead Capture Form. 98

3. Application Process. 98

4. Email Nurturing Campaigns. 99

5. Advertising. 99

Chapter 10: Top 10 Frequently Asked Questions. 101

1. What professions are suitable for having a signature book? 101

2. What if I don't have time to write a book? 101

3. What if I'm not a good writer? 102

4. What if I don't yet have enough to say, to write a book? 103

5. What if I don't know how to organize my book? 104

6. What if no one reads my book? 105

7. What if I don't plan to be an author? I'm just a business owner. 105

8. What if I don't have a publisher? 106

9. What if my business is too small for this method? 106

10. How can I make a lot of money from selling my book? 106

Conclusion. 108

Introduction

People have busier lives and shorter attention spans.

Competition is everywhere, thanks to the Internet.

And ads aren't as effective as they used to be.

Unless you're happy competing on price, or getting into a "features" arms race, "Me Too" Marketing just isn't good enough. Not anymore.

In "Plant Your Flag", you'll discover how you can very quickly:

1. Magnetize mediocre marketing,
2. Captivate the best clients, and
3. Go from hunting to becoming the hunted, in business.

Before you finish this book, you'll know more than 99% of people in your industry about:

- Writing the correct book

- Promoting it successfully

- And using it to have that kind of credibility and authority that creates an almost unending stream of leads and clients into your business

If you've ever felt like you were playing small in life...

- like you could be making a bigger impact...

- like you could be your serving people in a fashion that gets them REMARKABLE results every time...

- like you could be doing more with your time, talents, and treasures...

I'm glad you chose this book. In the next chapter, you're about to make another very important choice.

Bolaji

Chapter 1: The Chosen One.

The Bachelor.

Everyone wants to be the one chosen.

On the Bachelor, and countless other reality shows,

We empathize with the ones kicked off every week.

And are hopeful for the ones remaining.

We cringe when one lady (or guy) doesn't get the rose to move on to the next round.

Why? Because we all loathe rejection. It feels so personal. So permanent.

We all want to be the one chosen.

We dread the words: "You are the weakest link: Goodbye!"

We dread the words: "You're fired."

We all want to hear: "You're going to Hollywood."

That you get a rose and are moving on to the next round.

"The Chosen One" is actually a THING!

You'll see it in epic movies across the decades.

From Eddie Murphy's "The Golden Child" back in the 80s
to one of my contemporary favorites – Neo in "The Matrix".

Even in sports, you'll hear the language.

LeBron James.

LeBron James has it tattooed across his shoulder blades.

"The Chosen One."

And it's hard to argue with that self-assessment. According to Wikipedia.com:

- McDonald's National High-School Player of the Year.
- NBA Rookie of the Year.
- One-Time NBA Scoring Champion.
- Two-Time NBA All-Star Game Most Valuable Player.
- Two-Time Olympics Gold Medalist.
- Three-Time NBA Finals Most Valuable Player.
- Four-Time NBA Most Valuable Player.
- Five-Time All-NBA First Defensive Team.
- Ten-Time All-NBA First Team.
- Twelve-time NBA All-Star.

- 1st place All-Time in Career Assists by a Forward.
- 1st place All-Time All-Star Game Points Scored.
- Only player in NBA history to average at least 27 points, 7 rebounds, 6 assists for their career.
- **Three-Time NBA Champion.**

Wow.

James' net worth is estimated to be **$485 million USD**, according to TheRichest.com.

He's said publicly that he hopes to hit the $1 billion mark – a goal that so far only one athlete is believed to have achieved.

Michael Jordan.

Who wouldn't want to be the Chosen One???

Dan Gilbert.

Dan Gilbert is the owner of the Cleveland Cavaliers.

He's also the founder of Quicken Loans.

He became a household name when LeBron left the Cleveland Cavaliers in 2010, and "took his talents to South Beach." LeBron and Dan eventually made up. LeBron returned to Cleveland, to a King's welcome, and for a King's ransom.

Dan Gilbert's net worth?

$3.9 Billion USD, in 2015.

$5.4 Billion USD, in 2016, according to TheRichest.com

Gilbert is named by Forbes as one of the 500 richest businessmen in the world.

Each year LeBron plays for him, that number skyrockets at multiples of LeBron's net worth increase.

The Chosen One?

Or the one who chooses?

American Idol.

Here's a quiz for you.

How many winners of the American Idol can you rattle off?

- 2002: Kelly Clarkson. 3 Grammy Awards. Bonafide superstar.
- 2003: Ruben Studdard.

- 2004: Fantasia Barrino. 1 Grammy Award. Lifetime movie about herself.
- 2005: Carrie Underwood. 7 Grammy Awards.
- 2006: Okay, after 2005 the names get a lot less memorable. Maybe because I stopped watching at that point.

Some of these winners faded into obscurity.

Most of the non-winning participants did.

(Will Hung… Sanjaya… we miss you! You too, Justin Guarini.

And the kid who allegedly had a fling with Paula Abdul.

We heart you too.)

Some of these winners actually became bona fide stars.

"The Chosen Ones" of a new generation of pop stars.

So out of all these stars, which one's career would you most like to have?

No, not Carrie Underwood.

Don't get me wrong. To date, Carrie has earned:

- 17 Billboard Music Awards.
- Six consecutive Number 1 albums.
- Rolling Stone recognized her as the female vocalist of her generation (in any genre)
- Time recognized her as one of the 100 most influential people in the world
- Billboard recognized her as Country Music's reigning Queen.

So… not Carrie Underwood?

Nope. Not Carrie Underwood.

The right answer is?

(drum roll.)

 Simon Cowell.

(Yes, it was a trick questlon!)

The man who can't sing to save his life.

The ill-tempered man with 20,000 tight black t-shirts

 (Or was it the same one every time), who willfully and gleefully insulted his way into our living rooms. And our hearts. (Kind of.)

That Simon Cowell.

Simon was definitely not the Chosen One. Not by any stretch of the imagination.

But he got to choose the Chosen One.

Every season, there were new Chosen Ones.

And every year, there was Simon Cowell.

In 2013, and 2014, Simon Cowell's salary was $95 million dollars.

Each of those years.

His net worth back in March 2015 was $325 million dollars.

He's been a head judge on:

- Pop Idol (2001 – 2002)
- American Idol (2002 – 2010)
- The X-Factor UK (2004 – 2010)
- Britain's Got Talent (2007 -)
- The X-Factor USA (2001 – 2013)
- America's Got Talent (2016 -)

More importantly, he's produced:

- The entire Idol franchise (2002 -)
- The X-Factor franchise (2005 -)
- The Got Talent franchise (2007 -)
- The You Generation (2013 -)

Have you ever thought about what it would be like to be on THAT SIDE of the table?

You get to show up every show, look over the options, and dismiss the ones you don't want.

Everyone wants to be chosen BY YOU.

On reality TV, in professional sports, we'd rather be the choosers.

Ten times out of ten.

So why is it that in our business, we relegate ourselves to being a contestant on a reality show, all over again?

Why do we participate in "Me too" marketing, and succumb ourselves to the song-and-dance just so some judge (that we may not even care for) chooses us?

Isn't it past time to transition from being the hunter, to the hunted?

Isn't it past time to transition from being the chosen...

to the chooser?

Isn't it past time to choose yourself, plant your flag,

and let the best of the best compete to work with you?

It's time to PLANT YOUR FLAG, CLAIM YOUR MOUNTAIN,

BE THE BEST IN THE WORLD, and CHOOSE who gets to work with you.

Be the hunted.

Be the chooser.

Plant Your Flag.

Chapter 2: The Case Against "Me-Too" Marketing.

With so many choices out there, clients want to work with someone they KNOW, LIKE, and TRUST.

Commoditized markets. Shorter attention spans. Busier lives.

Multiple content engagement points – Smartphones. Laptops. Tablets.
eReaders. Blogs. Word of mouth. Books.
Conferences. Magazines. TV Shows.
And on, and on, and on.

Advertisements aren't as effective as they used to be.
(And they were never that effective, to begin with.)

Global competition, thanks to the Internet.

If you don't stand out, you'll be stuck practicing "Me too" marketing.

If you don't stand out, you will be stuck competing on price.

If customers don't understand why you are better,
they will continue to demand more at a lower price...
if they work with you at all.

But what's the alternative to what everyone else is doing??

- Marketing that stands out from the crowd.
- A way to be seen as a trusted advisor.
- A way to "zig" while everyone is "zagging".
- A way to transition from being the HUNTER to being the HUNTED.
- A way to simplify your Unique Selling Proposition (USP).
- A way to get your USP in front of the right decision-makers. Away from all the chatter.
- A way to help the right people KNOW, LIKE, and TRUST you.

But Who Is This For?

- Is your business in a competitive market?
- Do you have a decent customer lifetime value (More than $1,000 over the lifetime of each customer?)
- Are you trying to break into a new market… or establish your leadership in an existing one?
- Do you understand the value of differentiating from the competition?
- Do you already have a budget for differentiating yourself or branding?
- Do you read business books to educate yourself further about business?

If you answered yes to more than one of those, you'll appreciate what I'm about to share with you.

What Keeps You Up at Night?

- Are you frustrated with the boom-and-bust cycle of continuously hunting for new clients? Feast when you get a windfall of prospects, famine when you don't?
- Are you tired of having to cater to "bad clients", but keeping them because you can't afford to let them go?
- Are you frustrated with the fact that you can't tell which part of your ad budget is working, and which is a complete waste of money?

If so, your situation is more common than you might realize. While most would be loath to admit it to their competitors, a majority of businesses and business owners are worried that the money they're spending on ads isn't efficient. Or effective.

They're concerned that they'll always have to hustle for new clients. That they're one bad quarter away from dried up leads, and another crisis. That they'll never get off the entrepreneurial "hamster wheel".

I mean – business owners really just want marketing that makes SENSE.

Imagine This:
Imagine a business that runs smoothly without you having to hustle so hard every day.

No more chasing clients.

No more cow towing to "bad clients". You just work with the ones you like. You know - the ones who pay premium prices, on time, get results from working with you and are grateful for it.

No more competing on "the lowest price".

This works in virtually every profession, in every industry.

From Speakers to Salespeople.

From Coaches to Consultants.

from CEOs to Knowledge Experts.

Realtors. Lawyers. Corporate Executives. Service-Oriented Businesses.

If you need marketing, that helps you STAND OUT from the crowd...

A way to be seen as a trusted advisor...

A way to transition from being the HUNTER, to being the HUNTED,
this will revolutionize your business. Forever.

We're about to simplify your Unique Selling Proposition, and get it in front of the exact type of clients you want to work with. So they can KNOW, LIKE, and TRUST you.

Once you get them over that initial hump, you can become their trusted educator. Their marketplace advocate. And from there, the sky's the limit.

Bottom line?

You need something that will help you magnetize mediocre marketing, captivate the best clients, and become the hunted.

The secret weapon?

Become a recognized industry expert...

by publishing your very own signature book.

Chapter 3: The Signature Book.

Hang on. A signature BOOK?

I've heard of a signature brand… a signature fragrance… but a Signature Book?

"What is that?"

A signature book is a one-problem, one-solution book, written for one customer.

1 - One-Problem, One-Solution.

A Signature Book is a one-problem, one-solution book, written for one person.

That is the most succinct definition you will ever read.

And yet, there is a LOT packed in there.

Let's unpack it, just to make sure you understand what we're talking about here.

One Problem, One Solution:

You don't have to write an Encyclopedia on your industry.

Your prospects, customers, and clients have lots of problems.

Yes.

It's not your job to solve all of them.

You want to solve the biggest problem that you can competently and profitably solve, in a manner that differentiates you from the competition.

I'll give you an example.

For years, I've taken my cars to AAA Auto Care Car Center.

From oil changes to timing belt replacements, it's always been AAA Auto Care Car Center.

Recently, though, my wife got a coupon for a new place called 5-Minute Oil Change.

They do... Well... you get what they do.

Now all of a sudden, we get our oil changes done at 5-Minute Oil Change.

AAA will NEVER change oil as quickly as these guys do.

Guess what? We pay more for oil changes at 5-Minute Oil Change than we do at AAA.

But for clients like us, that are always pressed for time, that time savings is worth the premium.

And by the way, 5-Minute Oil Change gives free drinks while there and makes upsell recommendations (wipers, engine fluids, etc.) Some of which we take them up on.

I know you can solve more than one problem for your customer.
But let's write about 5-Minute Oil Changes.
Or more specifically to your industry, let's find that signature solution of yours –

The one you are known for (or want to be known for).
And let's write about that problem.

Let's attract the ideal client with that problem, and blow their minds with your signature solution.

Or – let's write a book about the problem that your entry-level offering solves.
The rest, they'll learn about after they engage with you.

2 – One Client.

So – we get the "One Problem, One Solution" bit.

But one person?

We're writing for one person?

Not literally… but go with me on this one.

Every business needs to have something called a CUSTOMER AVATAR.

I'm sure you've heard of this already. But as a refresher –

The customer avatar is a detailed description of your ideal client.

It's a representation of your best clients, wrapped up into one individual.

- Gender.
- Age.
- Name.
- Profession.
- Personality.
- Income level.
- Family demographics (married, single, divorced, kids, kids' ages, etc.)
- Hobbies.
- Quirks.
- Preferences.
- Type of service (s)he prefers to receive.
- Price sensitivity.

- Priorities related to their #1 problem, which you are helping them solve.
- ...And so on.

If you haven't actually written out a description of your customer avatar, you have to stop reading this RIGHT NOW, and take 10 or 15 minutes to imagine what this person looks like.

Actually, write it out – don't just think about it.

This single small activity will absolutely TRANSFORM your business.

(I've seen this happen more times than I can count.)

Seriously- if you haven't done this before – go do it now.

Once you go through this exercise, you'll really get the power of writing your Signature Book FOR THIS PERSON.

Now – realistically, your business services (and will service) folks that don't fit this description exactly.

But as you build more clarity around that Customer Avatar, that Ideal Paying Client, your marketing, your service offerings, your customer service, your operations, all of them will shift to better serve that customer avatar.

It may result in you firing some unsavory clients, even as you attract more and more of the type of client you enjoy. ☺

So – the Signature Book is ONE PROBLEM, ONE SOLUTION, for ONE PERSON.

3 - Tightly Focused.

A Signature Book is tightly focused on the value you provide.
It is NOT a text book.
It is NOT a comprehensive, in-depth dive into the industry.
It is not trying to solve world peace.
Neither is it trying to win any awards for length or weight.

We're not going for the "THUD" factor.
We don't have to impress prospects with the "girth" of the book, do we?
Truth be told, MOST BUSINESS BOOKS ARE NOT READ TO COMPLETION!

Why?

They're too darn long.

And the target audience for business books – business people – are some of the busiest folks on the planet.

So…. BREVITY IS KING.
Solve my problem in 15 minutes, not in 15 hours.
All I care about is that you solve my problem, in a manner that makes my life easier and less busy.

4 - Hello, World.

A Signature Book introduces the best of you to the world

5 - Customer Advocate.

It establishes you as an expert and authority in your niche.

But more than that.

It establishes you as someone who CARES ABOUT THE CUSTOMER.

How many of your competitors have taken the time to write out and publish AN ENTIRE BOOK on your customer's #1 problem?

6 - Try Before You Buy.

It gives a taste of what it's like to work with you.

7 - Lead Magnet.

A Signature Book generates leads for your broader business, in a MASSIVE WAY.

You've heard the term "generating leads in your sleep"? Imagine what it's like for people in your industry – reading your book at lunch time. At bed time. Keeping your book on their office desk. Or their night stand.

This is the most powerful type of INBOUND MARKETING there is.

Instead of dialing for dollars, you're BEING DIALED by people who want to give you money

.

Now, isn't that much more fun way to do business?

It gives you premium positioning in your industry as a customer advocate and customer educator.

Ten Undisputable Reasons You Need a Signature Book.

1 - Books are the new business card

2 - Advertising is dead.

3 - Position yourself as an expert.

4 - Position yourself as a problem solver.

PLANT YOUR FLAG

5 - Position yourself as an educator and advocate.

6 - Your competition isn't doing it.

7 - Leverage the book into media exposure.

8 - Charge higher prices.

9 - You get to stop chasing customers,

10- You get to fire bad, abusive customers,

11 - Be seen as the #1 authority in their niche.

12 - Clients will sleep better knowing you are a trusted authority and customer advocate.

They will brag about you. They will send you clients.

Chapter 4: Why You Can't Wait Six More Months.

You might think there isn't much urgency in your getting your message out.

In fact, there's more urgency than you know.

And it's not about you, either.

Here's the thing.

In a cutthroat, competitive marketplace, most businesses are focused on their own bottom line.

Which means that more often than not, if there is any distance between the customer's best interests and the bottom line... the customer's needs can get compromised.

You don't do that.

But a lot of your competitors, do.

So customers need someone to speak up for them, now.

They need someone to give them a voice in the local industry. Someone who will actually look out for their interests, and their bottom line. Someone who will shoot straight, tell them the truth, and not try to sell them a bridge they don't need.

Customers need someone to help them avoid common pitfalls.

To educate them on new trends. To tell them what's on the horizon. They need to tell them what to ignore, and what to take action on. They need YOU.

Here are 5 specific reasons why you need to FIND the right book, LAUNCH the right book, ACCESS your authority, and GATHER the right clients into your fold.

1. Someone needs you today:

    There is a customer out there that needs your help TODAY. In 6 months they will have asked someone else for help. Or given up completely.

2. You don't have to write the perfect book.

    You just need to solve a really focused but painful problem now.

    Think about this: An individual who calls 911 for an ambulance to pick them up, isn't going to spend time asking about the make and model of the ambulance. They won't be asking whether there's XM radio, or if they'll be stuck listening to FM/AM radio. They won't be asking any of those questions. They have a problem, and they want a solution – NOW.

Get your solution to these people that so desperately need it.

3. Imagine waiting another year, to think about that book.

How many business opportunities might you miss out on, in those twelve months?

How many leads?

How many clients?

How many speaking engagements, high ticket clients, and partnership opportunities?

How much more revenue could you have made in those twelve months?

There is a REAL COST to doing this LATER, versus NOW.

4. Would you like a better work-life balance now, or later?

   Imagine if your business was where you wanted to be.

   You are earning the income level you desire.

   You're getting the clients you desire.

   You're getting the publicity you desire.

   You're getting the speaking engagements you desire.

   How much easier would it be for you to spend time with family?

   Leave work at the office?

   Coach the kids' sports teams…

   or spend more time volunteering?

   Would that be worth stepping out of your comfort zone, to learn how to make this happen?

5. Your competition isn't waiting another twelve months.

   Your competition is not waiting six or twelve more months, to run their next big marketing campaign.

Your competition is not waiting six or twelve more months, to get that publicity. Your competition might not be writing a book… But they are making hay over the next six to twelve months.

You could keep fighting them head-to-head, tweaking "me-too" marketing tactics, and fighting for inches of progress.

Or. You could zig, while they zag.

Do it now.

Chapter 5: The F.L.A.G. Method.

1. Why you Need to Plant your FLAG.

Throughout history, men have "planted the flag" claiming ownership to territory, or land, in the name of their king, queen, country, or themselves. Planting the flag means staking a claim to ownership.

From mountain climbers to space explorers, planting your flag has huge ramifications.

How does that apply to business?

Let's take a closer look. But first:

2. The Great Space Race.

The year was 1957.

The Soviets had just shocked the United States by becoming the first nation to launch a satellite into orbit around the earth.

Sputnik, as it was called, frightened many Americans, who believed that the Soviets would soon develop an entirely new class of weapons that could be fired from space.

U.S. officials were especially concerned, for the success of

Sputnik was a direct rebuke to American claims of technological and scientific superiority over the communist regime in Russia.

It was a tremendous propaganda victory for the Soviets and gave them an edge in attracting less-developed nations into the Soviet orbit with promises of technological aid and assistance.

The United States responded by accelerating its own space program, and just months after Sputnik, an American satellite went into orbit.

In September 1959, the Soviets upped the ante considerably with the announcement that a rocket carrying the flag of the Soviet Union had crashed onto the moon's surface.

This was the first nation flag to reach the moon!

But it was an unmanned mission:

They couldn't plant their flag.

The Great Space Race reached a fevered pitch!

The U.S. redoubled their efforts.

On July 20, 1969, the United States' Apollo 11 became the first manned mission to land on the moon.

Neil Armstrong became the first man to walk on the moon. He and Buzz Aldrin deployed the American Flag on the lunar surface, a task that only took about 10 minutes but watched by the entire world.

A New Jersey-based company made the flag and sold it to NASA for $5.50.

The U.S. completed 6 successful manned landings on the moon - the last taking place in 1972.

The former Soviet Union subsequently attempted several landings unsuccessfully.

No human has walked on the moon since 1972.

No one from any other nation has walked on the moon.

The United States planted their flag on the moon...

Making NASA synonymous with space travel, the world over.

Where will you plant your flag?

3. The World's Tallest Mountain.

MOUNT EVEREST. 29,029 FEET.

"What's the world's tallest mountain?", I asked my 9-year old son.

"Mount Everest!", he immediately responded.

"Correct", I told him.

Buuuut... not so fast.

It turns out, that the true answer is: "It depends."

Mount Everest is the highest peak in the world above sea level. It stands at 8,848 meters (or 29,029 feet.)

First person to plant a flag at the peak?

Sir Edmund Hillary, in 1953.

Mount Everest is widely recognized as the world's tallest mountain.

In actuality, however, there's a mountain WAY taller than Mount Everest.

MAUNA KEA. 30,000 FEET.

Mauna Kea is a million-year old dormant volcano, on the island of Hawai'i.

Standing 4,207 meters (13,802 ft.) above sea level, its peak is the highest point in the state of Hawaii.

But don't be fooled - much of the mountain is under water.

When measured from its oceanic base, Mauna Kea is over 10,000 m (33,000 ft.) tall!

Making it the world's tallest mountain from base to summit, beating out even Mount Everest.

So how about that?

The world's tallest mountain is MAUNA KEA!

But – that wasn't fair. We had to go under water to find a taller mountain.

If we stay above ground, Mount Everest is the world's tallest mountain.

CHIMBORAZO. 1.2 miles taller than Everest….

According to Geology.com, Chimborazo in Ecuador has an altitude of 6,310 meters (20,703 feet).

Mount Everest has a higher altitude, and Mauna Kea is "taller."

However, Chimborazo has the distinction of being the "highest mountain above Earth's center."

This is because Earth is not a sphere - it is an oblate spheroid. As an oblate spheroid, Earth is widest at its equator. Chimborazo is just one-degree south of the equator. At that location, it is 6,384 kilometers (3,967 miles) above Earth's center or about 2 kilometers (about 1.2 miles) farther from Earth's center than Mount Everest.

So what's the point here?

Simply this.

1. **In business, as in with mountain peaks, you need to be seen as the best.**
   Mount Everest is by far the best-known mountain with that claim to fame. It's the toughest one to scale. We really shouldn't gloss over that fact. Mount Everest is not the tallest mountain by at least a couple of measures... BUT BY-AND-LARGE PEOPLE LOOK UP TO IT BECAUSE IT'S THE MOST DIFFICULT TO SCALE!

   Figure out what you want to be the best at. Better yet - -

   Figure out who your ideal audience is... what's most important to them... and see if you can be the best at any of those things they treasure.

By the most important measure, Mount Everest earns that number one spot.

2. **However, it's so important to note that there are many measures of "best".**
To people who live near Chimborazo in Ecuador, they probably have no need for Mount Everest! Chimborazo is #1 to them. And for the folks in Hawaii, they can always rest assured that they truly have the tallest mountain.

If Coca-Cola is the number one soda in the world, should all other sodas pack up and go home?
No. There are:
- Lemon-lime sodas.
- Orange sodas.
- Diet sodas.
- Cherry sodas.
- Root beers.
- Cream sodas.
- Strawberry sodas.
- Grape sodas.
- And on, and on, and on.

4. How Does This Apply to Business?

You can always find a way to be number one, to YOUR audience.

If you're a public speaker, and you want to be seen as #1 in the world… you can't try to do exactly what the current #1 in the world does. You have to segment your audience more finely… find out what THEY most need right, and specialize in a key slice, a key sliver of that need area.

Same thing applies if you're a CEO, a Consultant, a Coach, an Entrepreneur… whatever your calling.

The problem comes about when you:

- Don't know who your ideal paying clients are …
- Don't know what their top needs are…
- Don't know how you can meet those needs in a unique way.

In business, your audience needs you to plant your flag. To stake your claim.

I learned this the hard way, early in my career, after years of frustration with my advertising and marketing efforts.

I was tired of hustling for new clients, tired of serving clients who weren't an appropriate fit, tired of spending so much time introducing myself.

I was trying to provide services to anyone who could pay.

I was frustrated, burned out, and anxious.

And that's when I stumbled on the Plant Your FLAG method.

5. What is the Plant your F.L.A.G. Method?

The Plant the FLAG method entails publishing an authoritative book that shows that ideal client how to solve a key problem. It gets them from point A to point B... and demonstrates your commitment to being an advocate for their success.

It also lets them know how they can work further with you... IF they're a fit.

The four steps in the Plant Your F.L.A.G. Method are:

1. F: Find the Right Book.
2. L: Launch the Right Way.
3. A: Access the Right Authority.
4. G: Gather the Right Clients.

Let's get into each of those.

Chapter 6: F: FIND the Right Book.

I considered naming the first step "FINISH your Book."

Why?

Because many professionals in your position have already THOUGHT about (one day) writing a book. Maybe you've even got a few ideas jotted down somewhere.

But the thing is? Finishing isn't enough.

Finishing the wrong book is not only a poor use of your time, but it could also be VERY HARMFUL to your business. It could get you focusing on the wrong services... attracting the wrong clients... pursuing the wrong Unique Selling Proposition.

Think of it as climbing the wrong mountain.

You thought you were a few hundred feet up from the base of Mount Everest.

Instead, you find yourself a few hundred feet up from the base of Mauna Kea.

(That's underwater, by the way. Not good.)

So FINDING the right book is key.

"Well, how in the world do I FIND the right book?"

I'm glad you asked.

You're about to discover how to both FIND and FINISH the right book.

And it will take three separate phases to get there:

- Phase One: THE FINDING.
- Phase Two: THE FLESHING OUT.
- Phase Three: THE FINISHING.

Phase One: THE FINDING.

Here's the traditional way of writing a business book.

- Start with a blank page. (WRONG.)
- Start at the very beginning: *"I was born on a brisk Monday morning..."* (WRONG.)
- Create a quick 5-minute book outline on the back of a napkin. (WRONG.)
- Take the kitchen sink approach: *"I must include everything I know!"* (WRONG.)

All this does is lead you to tons of unanswered questions.

- *"How much personal stuff should I include?"*
- *"How much of my expertise should I share?"*
- *"Where do I start?"*

- *"How long should my book be?"*
- *"How do I know when I'm done?"*
- *"Is this interesting enough?"*
- *"What should I call the book?"*
- *"What in the world will I DO with the book, after it's done?"*

Forget the old way of starting your book.

I'm going to show you how to FIND the RIGHT BOOK, for the RIGHT AUDIENCE. In six easy steps.

The 6 Steps to Finding the Right Book for Your Right Audience.

1. What's your GOAL for the book?
2. Who is your IDEAL PAYING CUSTOMER?
3. What is the URGENT NEED / PROBLEM that you can help them solve?
4. How can you do this in a uniquely beneficial way to them (USP)?
5. Now, outline your book.
6. Finally, pick your title.

1: What's your GOAL for the book?

Seriously.

It seems like a "no-brainer" type of question. But there are actually several reasonable answers to this. And your response will determine the type of book you write.

So – what's your goal for this book?

- A. To sell lots of books, and make profits from royalties?
- B. For the personal satisfaction of being a published author?
- C. To finally share your life story?
- D. To generate leads?
- E. For expert positioning in your industry?
- F. To attract your ideal clients?
- G. To repel less-than-ideal clients?
  Or something else entirely?

Think about it.

Choose the options that honestly pertain to you.

I will tell you, that with the exception of A (making tons of profits from royalties), the rest are perfectly good answers.

The type of book I teach my clients to find and finish are signature books.

One problem, one solution books, written for one client – their ideal client.

So if you were my client, I would coach you to focus on **B, D, E, F,** and **G.**

Note: You CAN write a book about your life story. In fact, I recommend it!

In today's parlance, the publishing industry calls that a memoir.

It's less complete than an autobiography, but chock-full of anecdotes and lessons from a period of your life. Everyone, in business or otherwise, should write at least one memoir.

And if you're a motivational speaker, then your life story IS your product! So you definitely HAVE TO write a memoir.

But bear in mind that a SIGNATURE BOOK is shorter, and exclusively focused on your ideal client's NEEDS and PROBLEMS.

The Plant Your F.L.A.G. method is all about writing a signature book.

In some cases, clients of mine have combined a Memoir with a Signature Book.

That certainly takes more effort and time, but that's fine as well.

Take a moment, and write down your exact goals for this book.

You can't hit a target if you don't know where that target is.

Or... what the target is. For that matter.

"But what's with the repelling of clients?", you ask.

Great question. This one feels counter-intuitive to most people.

At first.

But consider this: There is an opportunity cost, for every client you serve. Meaning, for every client that ties up your time, attention, and resources, that's another client that you're now unable to serve.

We all subconsciously like to think we have an UNLIMITED CAPACITY to serve clients. "Keep 'em coming!", we say to ourselves. But the reality is that:

- Some customers are energy vampires.
- Some customers are price-hagglers.
- Some customers are never satisfied, despite our giving them the best.
- Some customers never stop second-guessing.
- Some customers want to comparison-shop.
- Some customers don't know what they want, and will keep changing the requirements.

And on, and on, and on.

Imagine you had the capacity to serve 10 clients well…

But you took the first 20 that came along.

How different would your day-to-day work experience be, with:

- 2 energy vampires
- 2 price hagglers
- 2 dissatisfied, disgruntled personalities

- 2 ideal customers (they somehow randomly snuck in there!)
- 2 customers that keep switching requirements on you?

...Versus 10 ideal customers?

A business mentor told me once that you can provide a business product or service along these three dimensions:

1. Better
2. Faster
3. Cheaper

It's always possible to deliver one out of those three...

Often possible to deliver any two out of those three...

But NEVER possible (or advisable anyway) to deliver all three.

I'll go a step further. And say you should NEVER focus on CHEAPER.

See what I did there?

If your business model is predicated on being the cheapest, I'm politely but firmly pushing you away.

I'd love to have you as a friend! But I don't want you as a client. Because you won't be able to appreciate my premium-priced services.

Focus on BETTER and FASTER.

Better yet – just focus on BETTER.

Leave FASTER your competition.

If you're actually solving your client's major problem EFFECTIVELY, THOROUGHLY and COMPLETELY...

They will be more than happy to give you a little extra time to see them through to the end of their headaches and worries.

Focus on better – and you don't have to compete to be the cheapest.

You don't have to rush, and risk doing shoddy work.

Or risk sacrificing your health in the process.

Do better.

And gently push away any customers that demand FASTER... or particularly... CHEAPER.

"But honestly – how do I figure out who my Ideal Paying Clients are?"

I'm glad you asked.

2: Who is your IDEAL PAYING CUSTOMER?

Here are some questions to help you narrow this down.

1. **What industry do you serve?**
   That's an easy enough one to answer.

2. **What are the top 10 products/services you provide to that industry?**
   Take your time. List them out.

3. **What are the 20% of items on that list that contribute about 80% of your profits?**
   As "for-profit" business goes, profitability is pretty high on the list of priorities.
   It's not everything, but if you can't keep the lights on, pay your staff, pay yourself, equip your company to provide top-notch services... everything runs to the ground pretty quickly.

4. **What are the most desirable categories of clients to serve in your industry?**
   - These are ones who DESPERATELY NEED those high margin services...
   - Ones that have a budget...
   - Ones that don't haggle on price...

- Ones with whom you'd actually enjoy interacting with on a daily basis.

Make a list of the most desirable categories of clients.

Note: Don't set yourself up as the expert of a lukewarm problem.

If you do, every day will be a battle to against mediocrity and procrastination with your clients.

Target clients where the house is burning down, and they need a fireman STAT.
If you do that, things get infinitely easier and more enjoyable for you.

Tell you what - let me illustrate that for you, in the next section.

3: What is the URGENT NEED / PROBLEM that you can help them solve?

Don't Sell Ice Cream in Baghdad.

As I was driving my six-year old off to camp for the day, a BBC report about a worldwide heatwave, came on the radio.

Apparently, England is experiencing temperatures of up to 36 ° Celsius (97 ° Fahrenheit.)

And the United States is experiencing temperatures of up to 38 ° Celsius (100.4 ° Fahrenheit.)

But in Baghdad? The temperature at the time of this report was **51 ° Celsius (124° Fahrenheit!)**

As I listened, a BBC reporter went on location, in Iraq. She visited a Street in Baghdad where vendors sell nothing but air conditioners, air coolers, and fans.

Once there, she immediately made a beeline for the first store and interviewed a couple of young Iraqi entrepreneurs. At the end of their conversation, the reporter asked them if they preferred the sweltering heat of summer time, or the cooler fall in September.

Through a translator, the young men laughed and said:
"No. No fall. We love hot weather. Good for business!"

A similar conversation occurred between the reporter and the owner of an ice cream shop.

Business was also booming at the frozen dessert saloon.

But then, the astute reporter asked a very important question. One that made me stop the car turn on my voice recorder and capture this story.

She asked the ice-cream shop owner:

"Do you think the ice cream helps people cool down?"

"No!", he answered through laughter. *"Nothing helps. It's too hot!"*

And there you have it.

Don't get me wrong - I bet almost everyone who walks by an ice-cream shop in 51 ° Celsius (124° Fahrenheit) weather, stops for a cone!

And while they're eating it (undoubtedly inside the AIR CONDITIONED SHOP), they will feel cooler. It certainly helps emotionally. A nice, cold sugar high? What a lovely treat.

But a few minutes later, back in the unbearable hot sun, it's almost as if that person never got relief to begin with.

Contrast that with an air conditioner.

The air conditioner would cost several hundred, or even a thousand times, more than an ice-cream cone.

But if you had just moved to Baghdad, and I offered you a half-priced high-quality ice-cream cone, or a fully-priced high-quality air conditioner... which would you buy?

And if you were a new entrepreneur in Baghdad, whose passion was keeping people comfortable in that oppressive heat, which would you rather sell?

- Ice-Cream (an affordable nice-to-have that EVERYONE can buy?), or
- Air Conditioners (a premium-priced product that not everyone can afford?)

Note: You could also choose to carry fans, for your less affluent customers.

Or better yet - partner with a fan company, and exchange referrals.)

If you lived in Baghdad, would you rather sell ice cream, and nice to have, or air conditioners, a must-have?

You've heard the saying: *"You can't sell Ice cubes to an Eskimo."*

Well. I wouldn't sell Ice Cream in Baghdad, either.

I'd sell Air Conditioners.

Don't just sell what you like to sell, divorced from the realities of what people need.

(Don't sell sweaters and jackets in Baghdad.)

But just as important is to not sell them what they might be lukewarm about, no pun intended.

(Don't sell ice cream in Baghdad.)

Sell them what they desperately, urgently need NOW.

Just do it better than everybody else.

What are their top 10 URGENT PROBLEMS that need solving NOW?

With the ice-cream versus air-conditioner allegory in mind, make a list of your Ideal Paying Client's TOP 10 URGENT PROBLEMS.

Don't worry if you don't provide those services right now. There's potential for you to partner with folks who do… or even for you to migrate your own business toward those "urgent problems".

So let's not limit the scope of this list to what we can currently do.

Let's find out what these desirable clients ACTUALLY NEED.

Make a list.

Now. For each of those 10 urgent problems, go back and fill in these details:

1. What's the nature of the specific problem?
2. When do they actually experience each of these problems?
3. Where else does each problem affect them negatively?
4. Why can't they solve each problem themselves?
5. How have they tried to solve this problem in the past, and failed?

4: How can you solve one or more of their URGENT PROBLEMS...
in a uniquely beneficial way to them?

Okay. You now thoroughly understand who your ideal client is, what their biggest problems are, and what kind of services you can (or would like to) provide to alleviate some of those problems for them.

Now let's figure out what mountain you need to climb.

Let's figure out where and how you need to PLANT YOUR FLAG.

Let's find out what these desirable clients ACTUALLY NEED.

Pick the one item on that list of 10 problems, that best suits your combination of priorities:

Ability to solve...

Desirability of customer...

Profitability of that service...

And so on.

How can you help the client solve that problem in a uniquely beneficial way?

Remember – we're not focusing on CHEAPER. We're not focusing on FASTER.

We're focusing on BETTER.

Here's an exercise that will help.

From the client's point-of-view: What would life look like without the suffering caused by that problem? Paint that picture for your client. Write it down. Reverse all the negatives associated with their huge, urgent, painful problem. WRITE IT DOWN.

In there, is your Unique Selling Proposition.

Focus on excelling where the client needs it the most... and you'll never have to chase a client another day in your life.

Define your secret sauce. KFC's Colonel Sanders' has NOTHING on you!

5: Now, outline your book.

That secret sauce you just discovered in the previous step?

That secret recipe?

Is going to become the outline for your book. ☺

I want you to define POINT A: Where your prospective client currently is. This is pretty much the problem statement from above – where your client is going through all the negative stuff.

Then write down POINT B: Where you've solved that problem completely and thoroughly. Include all the detail you came up with above.

The job of your book is going to be to get them from Point A to Point B, in 5-to-7 steps.

Go ahead and make a list of the steps, or milestones, required for them to get from Point A to Point B. Each of those will be a chapter.

Now. I want you to also brainstorm the top 10 Frequently Asked Questions your client is likely to ask. Make this list.

And finally – brainstorm the top 10 questions your client SHOULD be asking, but probably isn't thinking about. Make this list as well.

Finally – determine the CALL-TO-ACTION of your book.

You now have EVERYTHING you need for the RIGHT BOOK... tailor-made for the RIGHT CLIENT.

- Chapter 1: Introduction.

- Chapter 2: The Problem They're Experiencing... and the implications of that problem on them.

- Chapter 3: What life could look like AFTER the problem is completely solved.

- Chapter 4: A summary of your solution (It's ideal if you have a NAME for your method.)

- Chapter 5: Step 1 of your method.

- Chapter 6: Step 2 of your method.

- Chapter 7: Step 3 of your method.

- Chapter 8: Step 4 of your method.

- Chapter 9: Step 5 of your method.

- Chapter 10: Frequently Asked Questions.

- Chapter 11: Questions You Should Be Asking (But Probably Aren't.)

- Chapter 12: What to Do Next.

6: Finally, Pick Your Title.

Ah – the time of reckoning! You may have had a title in mind before…

But now that you truly understand your ideal client?

I mean, know them almost better than they know themselves?

Now that you understand the problem you will help them solve?

NOW – you can come up with a powerful title.

TITLE: The Problem You Help Them Solve.

This could also be the name of your method... but only if it serves the dual purpose of illustrating the problem / solution.

SUBTITLE: Your Unique Selling Proposition.

This is how you solve that problem in a unique way.

I recommend coming up with about 5 options for each... and then playing around with them, mixing-and-matching, until you land on a combination that REALLY hits the bullseye. If you can ask someone who matches your ideal client profile, do that.

Phase Two: THE FLESHING OUT.

Once you have all that research done, and you've actually FOUND the right book for the right audience, writing it is a breeze!

Except.

Except if you try to do it the traditional way.

The traditional way includes:

- Grinding it out...

- Suffering from writer's block…
- Lots of starts and stops…
- Frustration, pain, guilt, and more frustration…

This phase usually takes people 18-to-24 months, on their own.

We help our business clients get this phase done in a lot shorter amount of time than that.

Anywhere from 1-to-3 months.

Here's how it works:

Our publishing project manager interviews you over several sessions.

Each interview session is done over the phone, or via a web software like Skype or GoToMeeting.

For each item in your outline, you come up with 3-to-5 explanatory steps… and a story or anecdote to illustrate. It totally gets rid of the pressure of writer's block.

Each conversation could take anywhere from 20-to-45 minutes. These are fun conversations. You come with your bullet points, and considering this is material you already know back-and-forth, you just flow with it. Our project manager will occasionally ask follow-up questions, to get more insight on a particular aspect.

Painless. Profitable. Productive.

(Oh yeah. And Fun.)

Once all the chapters have been expounded upon via these audio interviews, our team gets the audio conversations transcribed.

You now have a very rough draft of the skeleton, or straw-man, of your book.

This is an exciting milestone!

Phase Three: THE FINISHING.

But you don't want to release a skeleton, or a straw man, to the world.

Oh no. We bring a team of professional writers onto the project for you, and convert that set of transcripts, into an actual business book.

Introductions, real paragraphs, bullet points, 3rd-party references and anecdotes, summaries of key points, conclusions, the whole thing. We make sure the book has well-structured, powerful sentences, without stripping the book of your voice and personality. This is very important.

Once the writing is completed, we run it to our professional proofreading and editing team, who get it all cleaned up. If you choose to do this process yourself, don't skip on the editing.

Design.

At this point, we enter the design phase.

Our publishing team gets the interior of your book formatted, for eReaders (like the Kindle), and for physical printing. We also get the book cover designed!

With the insides of the book done and the design completed, the next step is to run it to the printers and...

CONGRATULATIONS! YOU'RE NOW A PUBLISHED AUTHOR!

This is an AMAZING and AFFIRMING milestone for pretty much everyone!

So getting this far – you deserve a pat on the back.

And by the way – that book you just completed?

Is about the BLOW THE SOCKS OFF of your industry.

I guarantee it.

This whole process of FINDING and FINISHING the RIGHT BOOK has taken you about 3 months.

It's okay if it takes 4, 5, or 6 months even. The benefits you'll get from the book will last your entire career.

But all that wonderfulness is just the first step "F", in the F.L.A.G. method.

Remember: Plant your F.L.A.G. stands for:

1. **F**: FIND and FINISH the Right Book.
2. **L**: LAUNCH the Right Book.
3. **A**: ACCESS the Right Authority.
4. **G**: GATHER the Right Clients.

Let's now move on to "L: LAUNCH the Right Book."

Chapter 7: LAUNCH the Right Way.

Don't waste time and energy trying to figure this all out from scratch. There are countless books out there, good books, languishing in obscurity. Gathering cobwebs. To pull a successful book launch, you need to execute the RIGHT launch plan.

- Hitting PUBLISH on your book, once it's done, is NOT a launch plan.
- Neither is FRIENDS & FAMILY.
- Nor is HOPE.

My Associate Dean in business school, Dr. Kembrel Jones, would tell us students often:

"Hope is not a strategy."

"Well, how about I just submit my book to a traditional publisher, then?"

You could go that route.

If you talked to a traditional publisher, before they even considered taking you on, they'd ask whether you have a massive platform already. They'd want to know how big your email list and social media following are. They'd want to know that they were putting their weight behind a "SURE THING".

And can you blame them? Truth be told, traditional publishers aren't in the business of spending time and energy on very niche products. They need books that will sell to the masses in huge quantities.

That may be your book.

But chances are, if you've followed the Plant Your F.L.A.G. method, you don't have a book for the masses.

You have a book for your EXACT IDEAL PAYING CLIENT. The one out there who desperately needs your service, and, once she knows, likes, and trusts you, will become a very profitable long-term client.

What you need, is to publish direct-to-market.

SELF PUBLISHING – DONE CORRECTLY.

If you don't get this right, you'll be frustrated with flat line results, and your book could be a huge waste of time and money.

If you do get this right, this is predictable. You won't just be a published author; you'll be a bestselling author.

The launch phase has 7 steps:
1. Keyword Strategy.
2. Category Selection.

3. Book Title, Description & Cover.
4. Reviews.
5. Bestseller Launch.

1. Keyword Strategy.

People search on online book stores like Amazon, via keyword phrases.

Say you have an individual searching for something on business plans. They may use any of the following phrases to search for a reputable book on the subject:

- Business Plan
- Business Plan Templates
- Business Plans for Dummies
- Business Plan Writing
- Business Plan Writing Guide

You may have another individual searching for something on email marketing. They may use any of the following phrases to find the solution they need:

- Email Marketing
- Email Marketing – A Beginner's Guide
- Email Marketing Demystified
- Email Marketing Rules
- Email Marketing Blueprint
- Email Marketing Tips & Tricks

Let's go through another example. Branding. They may try:

- Branding
- Branding for Dummies
- Branding B2B
- Branding Yourself
- Branding Your Business

Interesting, right? Now, book marketplaces like Amazon allow you to specify a number of keywords with your book listing. This signals the search engine that your book is relevant when someone types in one of those search terms. So the idea is, by anticipating what keywords your IDEAL PAYING CLIENTS are using to search for solutions, you can ensure your book features those very keywords.

Thus putting you "eye level" on the digital shelves, so to speak.

Now – knowing this is one thing.

Executing it properly is another thing entirely. Why?

Because the vast majority of authors are simply GUESSING, when they select their keywords.

There are two problems with this approach:

1. **Wrong Keywords:**
   The keyword phrases you think your IDEAL PAYING CLIENTS are using to search, and what they're actually

using, could be miles apart.

You are not your customer. You may be similar to your customer in a lot of ways, but never assume that they would do what you would for.

For starters, even you match them exactly from a demographic standpoint, you are way more educated about the solution to their problem, than they are. Therefore, your guesses about how they might search are exactly that. GUESSES.

2. **Right Keywords, but Too Competitive:**
   Assuming you get lucky and are able to figure out one or two of the keywords they're using to search – ex- "BRANDING", or "BUSINESS PLAN". That generic keyword may be SO COMPETITIVE (so many different books using it), that even though you're on the "right shelf", your book is hidden behind 7 layers of other books on BRANDING.

Ideally, you want to have a good selection of "LONG-TAIL" keywords. These are more specific keyword phrases that your IDEAL PAYING CLIENT is using to search for a solution to their pain.

Without the right tools to find these keywords, it's like looking for a needle in a haystack.

Or better yet – looking for a specific piece of hay in a haystack. At least when you find a needle, you know you've found it. With guessing at keyword phrases, it's hard to know without testing every single keyword phrase for weeks at a time, when you've found the right combination.

For my clients, I use proprietary software tools to read through Amazon's API (Advanced Programming Interface), and determine what keywords are:

1. Relevant to your book
2. In high demand
3. But with moderate to low competition

What this does, is that it finds you the shelves at or close to eye level, where you can easily get to the front row.

By combining these kind of keywords (on Amazon's book store you get to specify up to seven keywords), you maximize your visibility to the right people, at the right time – when they're searching for a solution.

Done correctly – this creates fantastic visibility.

But if any of these steps are of course – HELLO OBSCURITY. HELLO CROWDED SHELVES.

2. Category Strategy.

Categories are of CRITICAL importance, in online bookstores like Amazon.com. Why? Because many people know the general category of book they're looking for, but may not quite know the keywords to use for their search. So they "browse by category".

Unfortunately for novice authors (but fortunately for YOU, because you're learning the inside track), there are hundreds and hundreds of categories and sub-categories to wade through!

If your IDEAL PAYING CLIENTS are searching for a solution in one sub-category, but your book is listed in an entirely different category… they and your book will be like ships passing in the night. One blissfully oblivious to the presence of the other. We can't afford that now, can we?

"So how difficult can choosing a category be??"

Well, just like with the keywords, guessing is likely going to leave you disappointed.

Let's say you've just published a cookbook.

And you're ready to put it in the "COOK BOOKS" category.

Well, here's what you'd be greeted with:

- Cookbooks, Food & Wine
    - Baking (8,837 books)
    - Canning & Preserving (1,251 books)
    - Cooking by Ingredient (6,835 books)

- Culinary Arts & Techniques (1,721 books)
- Drinks & Beverages (6,338 books)
- Gastronomy (2,691 books)
- Meals (9,765 books)
- Natural Foods (2,735 books)
- Outdoor Cooking (1,679 books)
- Professional Cooking (587 books)
- Quick and Easy (6,608 books)
- Reference (1,793 books)
- Regional & International (11,113 books)
- Special Appliances (2,865 books)
- Special Diet (14,743 books)
- Special Occasions (8,487 books)
- Vegan and Vegetarian (8,816 books)

TOTAL BOOKS IN THE CATEGORY COOKBOOKS, FOOD & WINE? 76,961.

YOU ARE ABOUT TO COMPETE AGAINST SEVENTY-SIX THOUSAND, NINE-HUNDRED AND SIXTY-ONE OTHER COOK BOOKS!

INSANITY!

It makes you want to not even bother publishing your cook book, doesn't it! How are you supposed to find visibility in that crowded field?!

That's why you list your book in sub-categories... not in the main category.

Now – even within those sub-categories, you're competing against at least

- 1,251 books (Canning & Preserving). Or
- 1,679 books (Outdoor Cooking).

That's still a really tall order! How do you gain visibility there?

The trick, is to find subcategories that have

- high demand (lots of people are clamoring for books in that category), but
- relatively low supply (there aren't that many books for these hungry buyers to buy.)

This is the process I help my clients figure out.

Solve this problem, and you're off to the races.

But, if you take the "spaghetti to the wall" approach – you might find yourself competing on the wrong end of 76,961 books.

3. Book Title, Description & Cover.

Once you've figured out your seven keywords, and your two book subcategories, you can now publish your book to the online bookstores!

This step is very straightforward. You simply visit the online book store and follow the instructions to list your book.

You'll need a few things before you can hit the "PUBLISH" button:

1. A well-crafted book title and sub-title
2. A professionally-designed book cover
3. A professionally-copy written book description
4. Your seven keywords
5. Your two book sub-categories
6. Your selected price point
7. A professionally edited and formatted book manuscript

Each of these items is of critical importance.

A Well-Crafted Book Title & Sub-Title.

Forget what the rest of the world thinks: Your book title has to speak directly to your IDEAL PAYING CLIENT. Remember – they're not buying WAR & PEACE. They're not buying A TALE OF TWO CITIES. They're buying your book because they have a specific problem, and they want a specific solution.

Your book title and sub-title need to communicate that.

A Professionally-Designed Book Cover:

Without a professionally-designed book cover, one that takes into consideration what readers in that genre want and expect, your book will end up D.O.A. (Dead On Arrival).

People ABSOLUTELY judge a book by its cover.

Forget all your amazing content – if your book cover is off, no one will ever get past page one.

A Professionally-Copy written Book Description:

Once the book cover and book title / sub-title hook them, they will now read the book description. If you have professional sales copywriting experience, then you can probably convey the most powerful message in one or two paragraphs, here.

But if you don't have that sales copywriting experience, be sure to get professional help.

Again, Book Title, Book Sub-Title, Book Cover, Book Description – these are all potential stumbling blocks that could turn away four, five, and six-figure clients before they ever get a chance to read your content.

You want to get these RIGHT.

Once you have these done, you can list your book on the online book stores, for a soft launch.

You'll notice that I listed this step a SOFT LAUNCH. That's because while we're putting the book onto the digital bookshelves, but we're not promoting it broadly. Not just yet. Before we officially tell the world that we're open for business, we want to get a handful of book reviews first.

So, let's talk about that.

4. Reviews:

Most authors struggle to get Book Reviews.

The reality is that less than 1% of book readers actually leave reviews. For some, it's an inconvenience. For others, they don't remember to. Whatever the reason, you can generally count on the fact that less than 1 out of every 100 people that read your book, will actually leave a review.

That's why you need a strategy for attaining those 5-to-10 book reviews before your bestseller book launch.

It's important for me to point out – you don't ever want to solicit fake or fraudulent reviews. Never, ever, ever. It probably goes without saying, but just in case, I'm putting it out there. You want individuals who have actually read your book, to leave a review.

One of the ways we do that, is by helping our authors set up an Advanced Readers Review Team.

Amazon.com and other book marketplaces allow authors to give free copies of their book, in exchange for an honest review. During the soft launch period, your Advanced Readers Review Team has the opportunity to get those reviews in for you.

That way, once you start advertising during the big launch, buyers can come in and be confident that your book is reviewed and well-reputed.

5. Bestseller Launch:

At this point, we're ready for THE BIG LAUNCH!

This is what we've been working toward all this time.

At Bold Publishing, we craft a custom launch plan for each of our clients – one that includes press releases, paid advertising, and promotion via email and social media. We coordinate all the tools at our disposal to create a wave of enthusiasm and support for your book during that launch week.

Our goal is to get your book into Bestseller Status on Amazon.com. So far, we've never failed to do so for any of our clients. **We have a 100% success rate.**

We have never failed. It's how we can offer money-back guarantees on our services.

Our services are not inexpensive. But we tell people - you will be a bestseller, or we will give you your money back. When you do this as often as we do, you can guarantee it.

Don't already have a massive audience?

Haven't yet built a sprawling online platform? No problem.

Unlike traditional publishers, we actually help you get to bestseller status, even when you're starting from square one.

Remember that hope is not a strategy. Not in business.

So all of this coordination:

- to identify the right client,
- to write the right book,
- to list it the right way on Amazon.com,
- to launch it the right way –

all these things, done correctly, establish you, the author, as a lifetime bestselling author in your field of expertise. And that, my friend, is when the fun really starts.

Being positioned as a Bestselling Author in your field works! In every genre you can think about.

It's working today, for people you've never heard of...that are only known in their industry.

If you don't get this right, your book will be a glorified business card.

PLANT YOUR FLAG

It won't get you massive PR, massive exposure, massive numbers of leads.

But if you do get it right, your book will get you on massive stages and get you're your dream clients.

What would it feel like to be on a stage in front of thousands of people there to hear you speak?

This is what you're about to unleash, by stepping up and Planting your F.L.A.G.

Chapter 8: ACCESS the Right Authority.

CONGRATULATIONS! YOU'RE A BESTSELLING AUTHOR!

And this is where the fun really starts.

- You're not just an expert in your field… maybe 20% of your competitors can probably claim that.
- You're not just a published author in your field… maybe 2% of your competitors can claim that.
- **You're a bestselling author in your field.** And that puts you in rarefied air.
  Fewer than one in a thousand, possibly fewer than one in ten thousand, will be able to claim that.

So now we need to let your industry, and your ideal clients, know that.

We already know you're an industry expert on the topic covered in your book.

But we want to make you a RECOGNIZED industry expert.

Now here's where most businesses unfortunately bet the farm on the wrong strategy.

- WRONG WAY TO GET RECOGNITION: Endorsing yourself (advertising.)
- RIGHT WAY TO GET RECOGNITION: 3rd-Party Endorsements.

Advertising is an age-old industry.

Most major businesses (and plenty of small ones too) spend most of their marketing budget on advertising. In fact, business people often equate advertising with marketing.

To get the industry to recognize your expertise, we need to do three things:

How to Become a Recognized Industry Expert through 3rd-Party Endorsements:

1. 3rd-Party Credibility from Press Releases.
2. 3rd-Party Credibility from Interviews.
3. 3rd-Party Credibility from Speaking from Stage.

1. 3rd-Party Credibility from Press Releases.

Press releases are largely misunderstood.

Press releases have long been a part of the marketing arsenal.

But using them the traditional way is a recipe for wasted money and disappointment.

Why most people fail with press releases:

1. Most people don't know what's newsworthy

2. Most people don't know how to distribute press releases
3. Most people don't know how to target press releases

I teach my clients to use press releases to sandwich their book release.

Ideally, they have:

Release 1: announce the book, and what it is about

Release 2: Celebrating the book as a bestseller.

Press releases give you the opportunity to build visibility for your book launch.

Done correctly, your release will be picked up online by local news media outlets.

What does that give you?

3rd-Party Endorsement.

3rd-Party Credibility.

Industry Authority.

But getting the format of the press release right is critical.

Having the press release say the right thing though, is everything.

It's the difference between wasted effort, and leveraged effort.

It includes:

- Focusing on your Unique Selling Proposition,
- Identifying and naming your Ideal Paying Client,
- Calling out the specific pain point that you address,
- Identifying how you solve that problem for that specific client,
- Contrasting yourself with your leading competition,

… and a few other absolutely critical things.

Write the RIGHT press release.

And then make sure it's visible in the RIGHT places.

2. 3rd-Party Credibility from Interviews.

I tell clients this all the time. And they get it – when they think about the experts they look up to.

Ask yourself this question:

"Do you listen to podcasts? If so, who do you listen to?"

TV and Radio used to be the only avenues upon which a subject matter expert could be interviewed, and broadcast their expertise to thousands.

Then Podcasts came along.

One day, as they say, everything changed.

I had the opportunity to learn directly from my podcast mentor, Entrepreneur On Fire (EOFire.com), John Lee Dumas.

John was able to from being a podcasting novice, to building a six-figure a month ($166,721.00 in July 2016) podcasting business.   John Lee Dumas has mastered podcasting.

As part of his high-level mastermind group, and through interviewing him on my podcast, I was able to crack the code on podcasting for branding and profits.

TV and Radio still carry a massively broader reach, all things being considered, but podcasts? Podcasts are WICKEDLY TARGETED in their audiences. They're like a radio station that only plays a very narrow kind of music, 24/7/365.

But I'll do one better than that.

With radio, everything is live. So when you tune in, even if the station only plays your 80s music, or country music, or news opinion... you have to listen to WHATEVER they happen to have on at that moment. Some you'll like, lots you won't.

With podcasts, listeners have the power.

They can listen to content that was broadcasted 3 months ago… or 3 days ago.

They can skip boring content… boring interviews… and get to yours.

(Yours won't be boring.)

Podcasts aren't just the future, they are the present, and everything else is yesterday's milk.

Don't get me wrong – TV and Radio as I mentioned are very valuable. But more so now from a branding standpoint. To be able to say: "I was on XYZ radio station, or XYZ local news. You get a BIG branding boost from doing that.

With podcasts though? Your ideal paying client is listening. Not just a random collection of people in a particular city, or state… but hundreds and hundreds, or thousands and thousands of ideal paying clients.

Saying: *"Okay. Here I am. You say you know my problem, and have a solution. Hit me."*

At Bold Publishing, we help our clients identify the podcasts catering to their Ideal Paying Clients. Then we help get them booked on those podcast shows – all by leveraging their bestselling author status, their existing area of expertise, their personal life story, and the 3rd-party credibility from our press release campaign.

It all ties together.

But only if you tie it together the right way.

3. 3rd-Party Credibility from the Stage.

Ah. Speaking from stage.

While some are comfortable with it, it sounds so distant, so fancy, so "other", to a lot of people.

The truth is, being invited to speak at any industry event, automatically positions you as an expert.

Why?

Well for one, you're not going to jump up in front of your peers, and prospective clients in your industry, without having something of value to add. So when people see you on stage, they know you're an expert.

Well if speaking from stage is so great, why don't more business owners do it?

Oh, that's an easy one.

It's because most business owners, despite being credible experts, have not yet mastered the art of getting invited to speak from anyone's stage. They haven't established themselves as recognized experts, and demonstrated that they are ready, willing and capable of adding value to an industry event.

So let's change that.

I had the opportunity to go through extensive speaker coaching with Toastmasters International, winning a few awards along the way.

I had the opportunity to study and work closely with the #1 personal development speaker in the world, Dr. Eric Thomas (E.T. the Hip Hop Preacher.).

And I've been fortunate to learn directly from the Internationally- renowned speaker and bestselling author, Brian Tracy.

I've also had the opportunity to speak from various conference stages, from Las Vegas, to North Carolina, and beyond.

Individuals' comfort level with addressing an audience from a place of authority (the stage, or the podium) will vary.

Bottom line though: If you're not comfortable speaking to audiences, either get coaching to build up your comfort level and ability, or hire someone to do it on behalf of your company.

One way or another, your brand's credibility will be stunted, unless someone is out there representing why and how you are the best in the world, for the specific type of client you most care about.

But when you put all those tools together:

Press Releases

Podcast Interviews

Speaking from Stage

You would have fully accessed the authority you deserve.

You will then be recognized as the best in your world, at what you do.

When that happens, all you need to do is to simply start accepting applications for clients who want to do business with you. At this point, you'll get to pick-and-choose.

Chapter 9: GATHER the Right Clients.

Gathering your clients entails having a scalable system to advertise, attract, and collect Ideal Paying Prospects.

You're essentially setting up your sales funnel. And yes, this includes advertising, but all of this sits on top of your now well-recognized expert brand.

The funnel should look something like this:

Traffic → Lead Magnet → Lead Capture Form → Application OR Email Nurturing → Sale

1. Lead Magnet.
2. Lead Capture Form.
3. Application Process.
4. Email Nurturing Campaigns.
5. Advertising.

Let's delve into each of these.

1. Lead Magnet.

What is a lead magnet?

A lead magnet is a free item, of value to your prospect that you give away in exchange for their contact information. It could be an eBook, a video training, a webinar recording, an audio training, or worksheet, a template, a piece of software, or something else of value.

2. Lead Capture Form.

What is a lead capture form?

A lead capture form is simply an online form that asks for that contact information.

Typically, you're asking for email address (as the bare minimum.)

You may also ask for the prospect's first name.

You want to minimize the number of pieces of information you request,
because the more data you request, the fewer people will go through will filling out your form.

3. Application Process.

Now this step can vary, depending on your business.

But usually, you want to give the prospect the opportunity to work with you.

However, setting this up as an application process, as opposed to blindly accepting any prospect that walks through the figurative door, positions you even more as the expert. It communicates that you don't just work with anyone off the street.

I help my clients set up an application process that not only asks the right qualifying questions to weed through tire kickers and price shoppers, but those questions also actually identify prospects that won't get great results based on their type of problem! That way, you only work with the folks whom you can really help, and whom you'll enjoy helping.

4. Email Nurturing Campaigns.

Not every prospect that goes through your lead capture form though, will be ready to work with you. Rather than throwing them back in the "ocean", you want to nurture them. I spent a decade doing this in my various corporate jobs, and it is a MASSIVE industry.

Email nurturing, or lead nurturing, is the glue that holds Marketing and Sales together.

For many people it can take 7 or more touches before they move from being a lead to a sale (customer).

Having a robust email nurturing campaign, using technology called email autoresponders, will allow you to continue to build the relationship with those warm leads... until they are ready to buy.

5. Advertising.

Once your funnel is set up, you can now profitably run targeted advertising.

As opposed to spending fairly blindly on advertising, or doing one-and-done advertising where you advertise your services for sale right off the bat... imagine the power of giving away something completely free in your advertising?

Much more compelling, right?

Now, advertising takes on a different meaning.

Chapter 10: Top 10 Frequently Asked Questions.

1. What professions are suitable for having a signature book?

The Plant your F.L.A.G. method works in just about any industry, for just about any profession.

But it's efficacy is super-charged, when your industry:

Is commoditized

Businesses are competing on price

Customers have a relatively high lifetime value
($1,000/customer is better than $5/customer)

If you're resigned to competing on price, then this method isn't for you.

But if you want to provide a high-quality, differentiated service,
and be compensated for it, then this will work in your industry.

2. What if I don't have time to write a book?

This is a real problem.

Most business books take 2 years or more to write.

The timeless book "Think and Grow Rich" actually took Napoleon Hill 25 years to write!

We help our authors start and complete their books in 1-to-3 months.

Whether it takes you 24 months, or 12 months, or 6, or even 3 months…

the dividends it will return to your business will be magnificent.

3. What if I'm not a good writer?

This is also a VERY REAL PROBLEM for many business owners!

You may not have written anything more than a few pages, since your days in school.

Now you're expected to write 50, 75, 100 pages, or more?

We found a lot of our business people, very credible experts in their field, struggling with the blinking cursor on that blank screen.

Writer's Block.

Realizing that a lot of business people struggle with this, I put together a process that works like gangbusters. And it can work for you as well. The secret is to NARRATE YOUR BOOK!

Narration gets rid of that "self-editing" voice in your head.

You're able to just flow with your ideas.

Even more effective than narrating into your cell phone, or on your laptop, is to have someone interview you.

Here at Bold Publishing, this is how we're able to extract the very best ideas from their heads, and onto the page.

4. What if I don't yet have enough to say, to write a book?

This questions trips a lot of business owners up.

"What if I'm not yet experienced enough?", or

"Maybe I should get a few more years' experience before writing a book."

The truth is, you don't have to be the world's #1 expert.

You don't have to be a world-renowned guru.

What do you have to be, is that person who is willing to help…

And you have to have a specific solution to a specific problem.

Think of it this way: If you saw a person walking in the desert, parched with thirst,

You'd be surprised what you know, what you take for granted, that others would gladly pay for.

5. What if I don't know how to organize my book?

Well, that's an easy one.

USE THIS BOOK! ☺

You're exactly the one we've written this book for.

6. What if no one reads my book?

    This is one of those subconscious thoughts that prevents us from trying.

    What if we fall?

    What if people see, and laugh at us?

    The great thing about writing a "Plant Your FLAG" book, is that even only a handful of people ever read your book, you will get exponential amounts of interest, credibility, and clients from people who HEAR about your book. Even without them reading it.

7. What if I don't plan to be an author? I'm just a business owner.

    I understand where this question is coming from.

    But by using the "Plant Your FLAG" approach, you don't have to do what typical authors do.
    You can stick to what you do best as a business owner, and work with my team to extract the information for the book, from your head, onto the page.

8. What if I don't have a publisher?

    No publisher? No problem. You've probably already learned by now from reading this book.

    Basically, you're much better of self-publishing to Amazon.com.

    But only if you do it THE RIGHT WAY.

9. What if my business is too small for this method?

There's no such thing as a company that's too small.

Now – your customers may not have a high enough Customer Lifetime Value ($1 vs $1000, for example), but even as a company of one… perhaps ESPECIALLY as a small company, using a "Plant Your FLAG" book to establish your industry credibility is CRUCIAL.

10. How can I make a lot of money from selling my book?

The interesting thing about it is that you're not trying to make a lot of money from selling your book!

Counter-intuitive?

Perhaps.

But this isn't about selling tons of books, or earning lots of book royalties.

This is about identifying your ideal paying client, identifying their biggest, most painful need that you can help them fix, and communicating your ability to fix that problem to that ideal paying client.

Once you're there, you want to be recognized as an industry expert, and a valued educator.

This industry credibility will give you the ability to attract and retain the exact kind of clients you want, doing the kind of work you are amazing at.

Conclusion.

People have busier lives and shorter attention spans.

Competition is everywhere, thanks to the Internet.

And ads aren't as effective as they used to be.

Unless you're happy competing on price, or getting into a "features" arms race, "Me Too" Marketing just isn't good enough. Not anymore.

In learning the "Plant Your F.L.A.G." method, you've discovered how you can very quickly:

1. Magnetize mediocre marketing,
2. Captivate the best clients, and
3. Go from hunting to becoming the hunted, in business.

You now know more than 99% of people in your industry about:

- Writing the correct book

- Promoting it successfully

- And using that book to generate the kind of credibility and authority that creates an almost unending stream of leads and clients into your business.

If you've ever felt like you were playing small in life...

 - like you could be making a bigger impact...

 - like you could be your serving people in a fashion that gets them REMARKABLE results every time...

 - like you could be doing more with your time, talents, and treasures...

You're now educated. You're now informed.

The next choice is yours.

Your audience needs you to WRITE, PUBLISH, AND LAUNCH THAT BOOK!

Need help?

From time-to-time, I open up 20-minute strategy consultations for credible experts who are ready to Plant their FLAG.

Click below to receive more information about the 20-minute strategy consultation.

http://www.BoldPublishing.com/strategy

I can't wait to salute <u>you as</u> your industry's next bestselling author!

GO PLANT YOUR FLAG.

www.ingramcontent.com/pod-product-compliance
Lightning Source LLC
Chambersburg PA
CBHW070325190526
45169CB00005B/1747